THIS BOOK IS FOR

BORN

LOTS OF LOVE
FORVER & ALWAYS

Made in the USA
Monee, IL
06 August 2020

37712944R00085